OUR SOLAR SYSTEM

Moon

BY DANA MEACHEN RAU

Content Adviser: Dr. Stanley P. Jones, Assistant Director, Washington, D.C., Operations, NASA Classroom of the Future

Science Adviser: Terrence E. Young Jr., M.Ed., M.L.S., Jefferson Parish (La.) Public Schools

Reading Adviser: Dr. Linda D. Labbo, Department of Reading Education, College of Education, The University of Georgia

COMPASS POINT BOOKS

MINNEAPOLIS, MINNESOTA

Compass Point Books
3109 West 50th Street, #115
Minneapolis, MN 55410

Visit Compass Point Books on the Internet at *www.compasspointbooks.com*
or e-mail your request to *custserv@compasspointbooks.com*

Photographs ©: PhotoDisc, cover, 1, 5, 6 (top), 11, 13 (top), 15 (top); DigitalVision, 3, 4, 7, 9, 14; NASA photo courtesy of Space Images, 6 (bottom); Scala/Art Resource, N.Y., 8 (left); Stock Montage, 8 (right); Stocktrek/Corbis, 9; NASA, 15 (bottom), 16, 18, 19 (bottom), 20, 21; Digital Stock, 17; Corbis, 19 (top); Guy Motil/Corbis, 22–23; Roger Ressmeyer/Corbis, 24–25.

Editors: E. Russell Primm, Emily J. Dolbear, and Catherine Neitge
Photo Researchers: Svetlana Zhurkina and Marcie Spence
Photo Selector: Linda S. Koutris
Designer: The Design Lab
Illustrator: Graphicstock

Library of Congress Cataloging-in-Publication Data
Rau, Dana Meachen, 1971–
   The moon / by Dana Rau.
      p. cm. — (Our solar system)
 Summary: Describes the formation, orbit, surface features, exploration, and future study of our moon. Includes bibliographical references and index.
   ISBN 0-7565-0438-4 (hardcover)
   1. Moon—Juvenile literature. [1. Moon.] I. Title.
   QB582 .R38 2003
   523.3—dc21   2002009938

Table of Contents

NOTE: In this book, words that are defined in the glossary are in **bold** the first time they appear in the text.

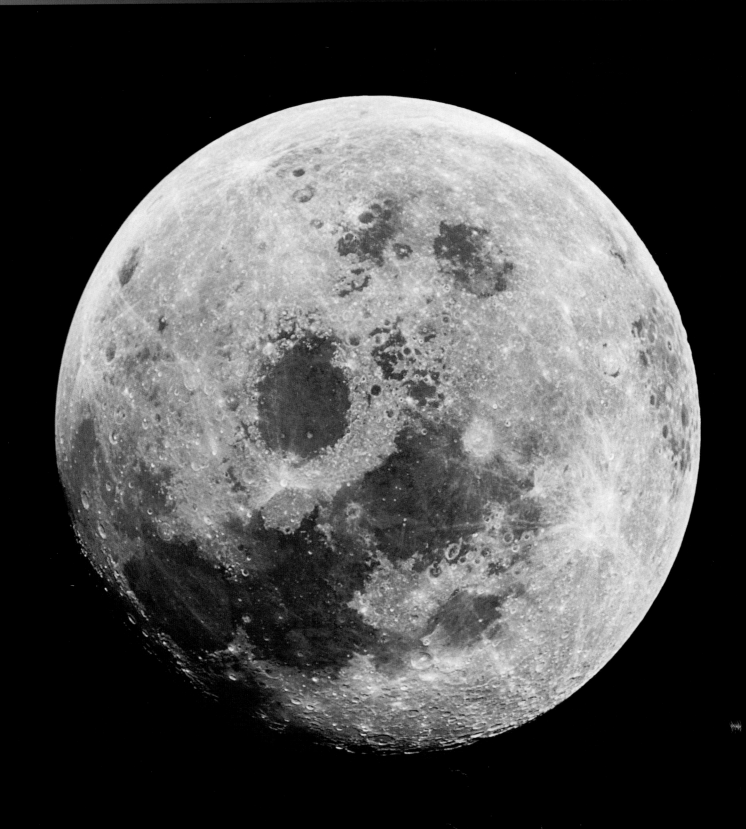

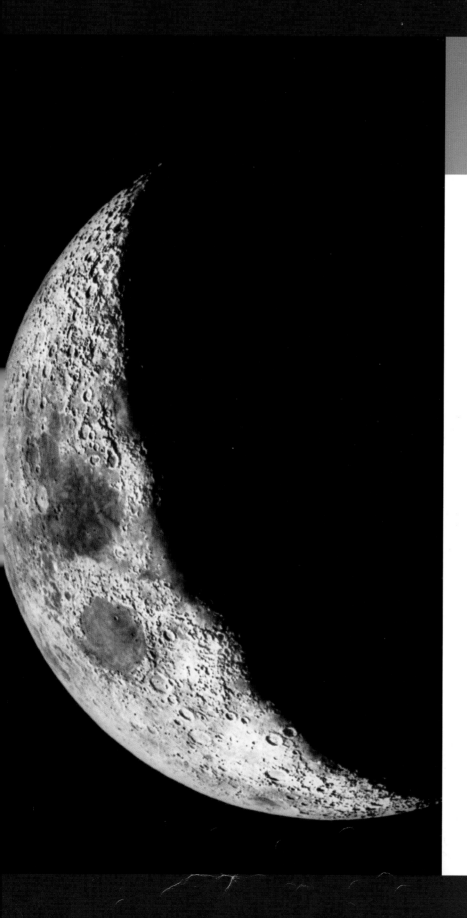

Looking up at the Moon

✦ Have you ever seen the man in the Moon? Some people think the dark and light patches on the Moon make it look like it has a face. People have created many stories and songs about the Moon.

The solar system is made up of nine planets and their moons. Other objects floating through space also make up the solar system. They are called comets, asteroids, and meteoroids. Many of the

◄◄ *Many people believe that the dark patches on the Moon make it look like a face.*

◄ *The Moon is the subject of many ideas, stories, and songs.*

planets have moons. Moons are also called **satellites**. Earth has only one natural satellite. Mars has two. Uranus has twenty-one natural satellites!

Most planets are large compared to the size of their moons. If Earth and the Moon were held side by side, four Moons would fit across Earth. Earth's Moon is the fifth largest moon in the solar system.

Ever since there have been people on Earth, they have been watching the Moon. Long ago, the Romans had a goddess of the Moon called

Comets (shown above in a computer ▶
enhanced view) and planets and their
moons (below) are part of our solar system.

Earth's Moon is the fifth-largest ▶▶
in the solar system.

Luna. In the 1600s, telescopes were invented. Astronomers, such as Galileo Galilei (1564–1642), studied the Moon with them. In the mid-1950s, astronomers began to study the Moon with spacecraft.

Galileo was ▶ an Italian astronomer who used this telescope to study the Moon.

Looking at How the Moon Moves

✦ All planets, including Earth, travel around the Sun, or revolve, in paths called orbits. The Moon travels in an orbit around Earth. While the Moon orbits, it also rotates, or spins.

It takes the Moon a little more than twenty-seven days to orbit Earth. This time is about the same that it takes the Moon to rotate once. This means that on Earth, people always see the same side of the Moon.

◀ *The Moon at various stages of its orbit around Earth*

People didn't know what the other side looked like. Spacecraft were sent to take pictures of it in the late 1950s.

The way the Moon moves in its orbit also makes the Moon seem to change shape. From Earth, the Moon does not always look like a round ball. It goes through **phases**. Over a month, the Moon seems to grow larger until it is round. Then it seems to grow smaller until it seems to disappear.

Half of the Moon is lit by the Sun at one time. From Earth, only part of the Moon's lit side can be seen. This is why the Moon's shape seems to change in the sky. When the Moon is a round shape, it is called a full moon. It sometimes has a curved shape. This is called a crescent moon. Sometimes none of the Moon's lit side can be seen. This is called a new moon.

The Moon goes through different ▶
phases over one month.

Looking at How the Moon Formed

⭐ Most astronomers believe that the solar system formed nearly 5 billion years ago. Astronomers believe that the Moon was formed about 4 billion years ago. They think that a huge object (about the size of the planet Mars) crashed into Earth while it was forming. This crash sent a lot

Scientists believe an object the size of Mars (pictured here) crashed into Earth billions of years ago. (Mars is the third-smallest planet.)

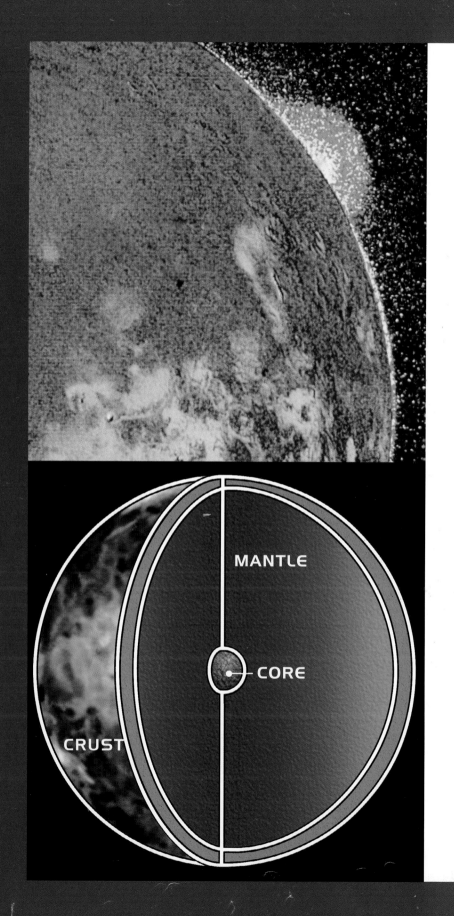

of material into space. Some of the material clumped together and formed the Moon.

After the Moon formed, there were many volcanoes on its surface. Volcanoes are mountains that shoot out hot, liquid rock called lava. When the Moon cooled, a hard outer layer called the crust formed on the surface. Below the crust is an area called the mantle. It is filled with heavy rock. Some of this rock is liquid. The inside of the Moon is still very hot. Some astronomers think it

▲ *Volcanic eruptions occurred on Jupiter's moon, Io (above). Similar eruptions occurred on Earth's Moon.*

may have a hard center made of iron. The center is called the core.

When the Moon was forming, it was also hit with meteoroids and comets. They crashed all over the surface of the Moon. They left behind holes called craters. The Moon has many craters dotting its surface.

There is still some activity on the Moon. Small moonquakes, like earthquakes, occur very often on the Moon. They are not very strong, however.

Meteors and comets hit the Moon to form craters like this one.

Looking at the Moon's Surface

The Moon is covered with light and dark areas. The light areas are lunar highlands. The dark areas are craters that were filled with lava when volcanoes erupted billions of years ago. The largest crater in the solar system can be found on the Moon. It is called South Pole-Aitken. This crater is 1,398 miles (2,250 kilometers) wide. It is 7 miles (11 km) deep. The Moon is covered by a mixture of fine dust and

▲ The light and dark areas of the Moon mark highlands and areas filled by lava billions of years ago.

◀ The South Pole-Aitken Crater

rocks. The dust and rocks were left behind after meteors hit the Moon.

An atmosphere is the mixture of gases that surrounds a planet. Atmospheres protect planets from meteorites. They are meteoroids that hit the surface of a moon or planet. A large number of meteoroids enter Earth's atmosphere every day. They burn up in the atmosphere before they reach the ground. The Moon has little or no atmosphere. All of the meteorites crash into it. They leave behind craters. That is why there are so many craters on the Moon. Some craters are small. Others are very large.

An atmosphere also creates weather on a planet. Without an atmosphere, the Moon has no weather. There is no wind or rain to erode, or break down, the craters. The surface of

There is no harsh weather on the Moon to erode its craters.

the Moon has not changed in billions of years.

Without an atmosphere, the Moon also has no protection from the Sun's harmful rays. When astronauts visited the Moon, they had to wear special suits to protect them.

Temperatures on the Moon can be extreme. During the day, the Moon's temperature can be as high as 225 degrees Fahrenheit (107 degrees Celsius). At night, the temperature can go as low as –243 degrees F (–153 degrees C).

◀ *An astronaut wears a special space suit to walk on the Moon.*

Looking at the Moon with Spacecraft

✦ For years, astronomers watched the Moon in the sky. They looked at it through their telescopes. Still, they were curious to know more about the Moon. They wanted to visit it.

On September 12, 1962, U.S. President John F. Kennedy made an important speech. He said that he wanted to send people to the Moon before 1970. The National Aeronautics and Space Administration (NASA)

John F. Kennedy wanted to send ▸
Americans to the Moon before 1970.

is the part of the government in charge of studying space. After Kennedy's speech, NASA got to work.

NASA built many rockets and spacecraft. Astronauts were trained. The astronauts practiced "walking" in space and flying the spacecraft. By 1969, everyone was ready to send a mission to the Moon.

On July 20, 1969, *Apollo 11* astronauts Neil Armstrong and Buzz Aldrin landed on the Moon. They collected Moon rocks. NASA continued to send Americans to the Moon until

▲ *An astronaut "walking" in space*

◀ *Neil Armstrong and Buzz Aldrin walked on the Moon in 1969.*

1972. In all, twelve men walked on the Moon.

Not all spacecraft sent to the Moon have astronauts. Those without astronauts are called unmanned missions. The Soviet Union (now Russia) sent many spacecraft to the Moon to take pictures and to collect samples.

In 1994, the U.S. spacecraft *Clementine* orbited the Moon. It photographed the Moon so astronomers could make maps of its surface. In 1998 and 1999, NASA's *Lunar Prospector* also orbited the Moon. It found ice

Clementine's voyage helped astronomers make maps of the Moon's surface. ▼

deep inside the craters at the very top and very bottom of the Moon, called its **poles**. Until this mission, astronomers didn't know that there was water on the Moon. The *Lunar Prospector* orbited the Moon for eighteen months. Then astronomers directed it to crash into a crater near the Moon's south pole. Astronomers were hoping that information from this crash would tell them more about ice on the Moon.

▲ *The* Lunar Prospector *orbited the Moon for eighteen months.*

Looking at the Moon from Earth

Have you ever looked at a full moon in the sky? The Moon looks round and bright. It seems to glow. The Moon does not give off its own light. The Sun is the only source of light in the solar system. Its light bounces off the Moon to create moonlight.

The Moon is not just an object floating in space to look at and to study. The Moon also has power over Earth. As the Moon orbits Earth, the Moon and Earth pull on each other. This is because both the Moon and Earth have gravity.

Gravity is a force that pulls objects to the center of a planet or moon. The Moon's gravity pulls on Earth. Earth's gravity pulls on the Moon. This pull of Earth and the Moon causes tides in the oceans on Earth. Tides happen when the water pulls away from the shore and then comes back again.

Earth's water on the side closest to the Moon is pulled toward the Moon. When water is pulled away from the shores, it is called low tide. When the water goes back, it is high tide. High tides and low tides happen twice a day.

◀ *Ocean tides are caused by the gravitational pull of both Earth and the Moon.*

Looking to the Future

✧ The Moon is the only place in the solar system that people have visited. Astronomers still want to know more about it.

Scientists continue to study the Moon rocks brought back to Earth by the U.S. and Soviet missions to the Moon. The rocks on the Moon have not changed for billions of years. Astronomers study the Moon rocks to learn more about the beginning of the solar system.

Moon rocks hold the key to many questions scientists have about our solar system. ▶

There have been more than seventy missions to the Moon. There are more missions planned. Some missions will have astronauts. Others will be unmanned. Astronomers have even talked about creating a Moon base. This would be a place on the Moon where people could live. They would study the solar system from there. Would you like to live on the Moon?

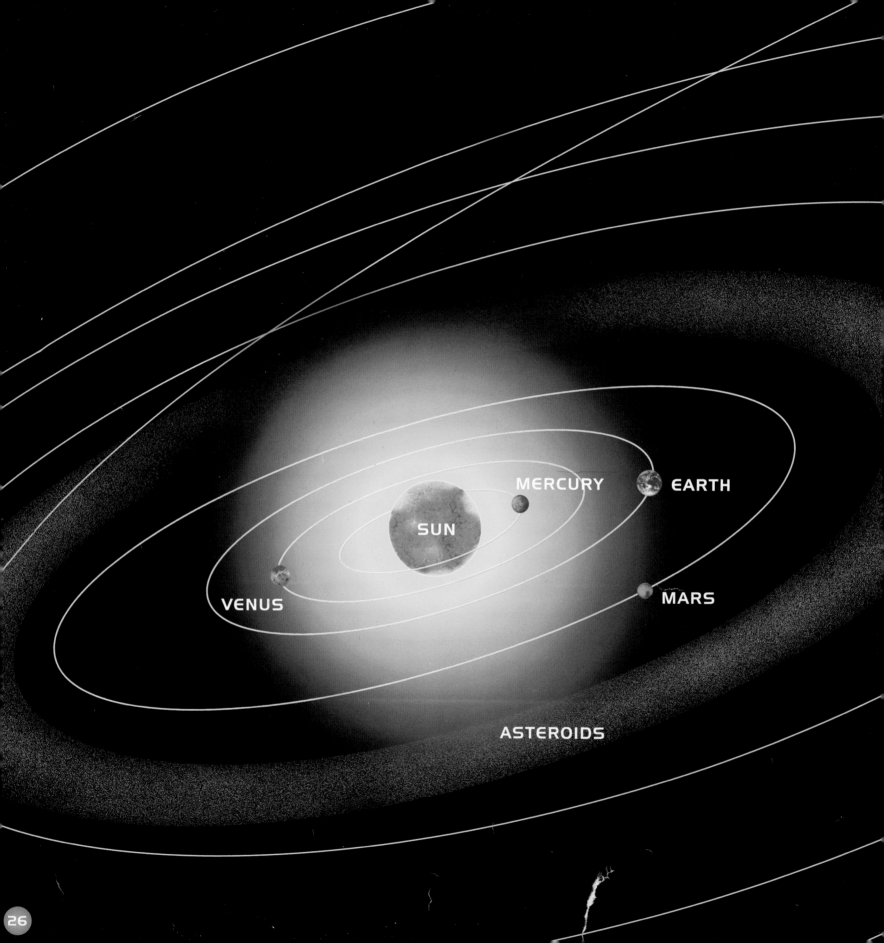

SUN

MERCURY

EARTH

VENUS

MARS

ASTEROIDS

JUPITER

URANUS

SATURN

NEPTUNE

PLUTO

Glossary

asteroids—chunks of rock that orbit the Sun, especially between the orbits of Mars and Jupiter

astronomers—people who study space

comets—pieces of ice and rock that have long tails of dust and orbit the Sun

meteoroids—chunks of rock in space; when they hit a planet, they are called meteorites

phases—the appearances of the Moon as seen from Earth

poles—the northernmost and southernmost points on the Moon

satellites—objects that orbit a planet

telescopes—tools astronomers use to make objects look closer

temperatures—how hot or cold something is

A Moon Flyby

If you weighed 80 pounds (36 kg) on Earth, you would weigh 13 pounds (6 kg) on the Moon.

Average distance from Earth: 239,906 miles (386,000 km)

Diameter: 2,160 miles (3,475 km)

Density (Earth=5,520 kg/m3): 3,341 kg/m3

Time it takes to orbit Earth: 27.32 Earth-days

Time it takes to rotate: 29.5 Earth-days (from new moon to new moon)

Did You Know?

- Most of the craters on the side of the Moon facing Earth are named for famous scientists.

- The Moon is not completely round. It is egg-shaped. The small end of the egg shape points toward Earth.

- Because the Moon has little or no atmosphere, its sky is always black, even during the day.

- In 1959, the Soviet *Luna 2* was the first spacecraft to visit the Moon.

- The U.S. *Apollo* missions and the Soviet *Luna* missions brought 842 pounds (382 kilograms) of Moon rocks and soil back to Earth for scientists to study.

- A total of twelve astronauts have walked on the Moon. Neil Armstrong was the first, and Eugene Cernan was the last.

Structure: rocky crust, partly liquid mantle, and possibly a rocky core

Average surface temperature: 225º F (107º C) day to −243º F (−153º C) night

Atmosphere: little or none

Want to Know More?

AT THE LIBRARY

Gibbons, Gail. *The Moon Book*. New York: Holiday House, 1998.

Lassieur, Allison. *The Moon*. Danbury, Conn.: Children's Press, 2000.

Mitton, Jacqueline and Simon Mitton. *Scholastic Encyclopedia of Space*. New York: Scholastic Reference, 1998.

Redfern, Martin. *The Kingfisher Young People's Book of Space*. New York: Kingfisher, 1998.

ON THE WEB

Apollo to the Moon
http://www.nasm.edu/galleries/attm/attm.html
For information about the National Air and Space Museum's exhibit on the *Apollo* missions

Everything You Ever Wanted to Know About the Moon
http://www.tsgc.utexas.edu/everything/moon/
For fun factoids, a list of missions, and general information about the Moon

Exploring the Moon
http://www.lpi.usra.edu
For information about the many missions to the Moon

The Nine Planets: The Moon
http://www.seds.org/nineplanets/nineplanets/moon.html
For a tour of the solar system, including the planets and their moons

Solar System Exploration: The Moon
http://sse.jpl.nasa.gov/features/planets/moon/moon.html
For more information about the Moon and related links to other sites

Space Kids
http://spacekids.hq.nasa.gov
NASA's space science site designed just for kids

Space.com
http://www.space.com
For the latest news about everything to do with space

Star Date Online: The Moon
http://www.stardate.org/resources/ssguide/moon.html
For an overview of the Moon

THROUGH THE MAIL

Goddard Space Flight Center
Code 130, Public Affairs Office
Greenbelt, MD 20771
To learn more about space exploration

Jet Propulsion Laboratory
4800 Oak Grove Drive
Pasadena, CA 91109
818/354-4321
To learn more about the
spacecraft missions

Lunar and Planetary Institute
3600 Bay Area Boulevard
Houston, TX 77058
To learn more about the planets

Space Science Division
NASA Ames Research Center
Moffet Field, CA 94035
To learn more about solar
system exploration

ON THE ROAD

**Adler Planetarium and
Astronomy Museum**
1300 S. Lake Shore Drive
Chicago, IL 60605-2403
312/922-STAR
To visit the oldest planetarium
in the Western Hemisphere

**_Exploring the Planets_ and
Where Next, Columbus?**
National Air and Space Museum
7th and Independence Avenue, S.W.
Washington, DC 20560
202/357-2700
To learn more about the solar system and
space exploration at this museum exhibit

**Rose Center for Earth and
Space/Hayden Planetarium**
Central Park West at 79th Street
New York, NY 10024-5192
212/769-5100
To visit this new planetarium and learn
more about the solar system

UCO/Lick Observatory
University of California
Santa Cruz, CA 95064
831/459-2513
To see the telescope that was used to
discover the first planets outside of our
solar system

Index

◀ **About the Author:** *Dana Meachen Rau loves to study space. Her office walls are covered with pictures of planets, astronauts, and spacecraft. She also likes to look up at the sky with her telescope and write poems about what she sees. Ms. Rau is the author of more than seventy-five books for children, including nonfiction, biographies, storybooks, and early readers. She lives in Burlington, Connecticut, with her husband, Chris, and children, Charlie and Allison.*